DEDICATION

To Finn and Asher, my two sons. I hope you always remember that you are enough.

ACKNOWLEDGMENTS

A special thanks to my family and friends and especially my wife for helping me learn that "I am enough".

In life there are storms and the seas can be rough.

You are you and that's enough.

People will tease you, call you names, and make you cry.

You will make mistakes, have accidents, and tell lies.

You will be told you are bad, you're no good and all kinds of means stuff.

You are you and that's enough.

You might get bad grades, break some rules, get in fights.

You will push people to their limits, argue, you won't always be right.

Just do all that you can, hang in there, never give up.

You are you and that's enough.

You might like to give hugs, kisses or just wave goodbye.

You might be out going, quiet, sometimes you feel shy.

Sometimes you will be cranky, grumpy and gruff.

One thing is for certain, you are you and that's enough.

Everyone is different: Color, shape, height, and size

If you try your hardest you might not win a prize.

In life there are storms, hang on tight; it's going to get rough.

You are you and that's enough.

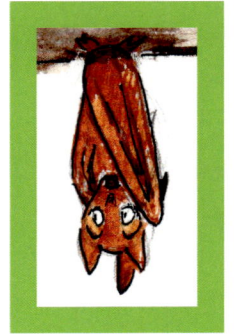

The End

Made in the USA
Lexington, KY
06 December 2017